# CONTENTS

Giving the Nazi salute in
the Reichstag (parliament).

# A NEW ERA FOR GERMANY

Below: Paul von Hindenburg, president of Germany 1925-34, in traditional military uniform. Opposite: Adolf Hitler, the new chancellor, in the uniform of the Nazi Party.

For those Germans who knew their history, 21 March was an important day. On 21 March in 1871, Chancellor Otto von Bismarck had opened the first parliament (Reichstag) of the new state of Germany. This state had been created by the unification of the powerful kingdom of Prussia and its smaller neighbours. 21 March was also the first day of spring and so it was a day that symbolized hope and renewal.

Sixty-two years later, on 21 March 1933, a fresh chapter of German history was set to begin. A new session of the Reichstag was to be opened. Unfortunately, the parliament building in Berlin had recently been burned down – by a Dutch communist, it was said. So the opening ceremony was to take place in a church, the Potsdam Garrison Church, on the outskirts of Berlin. It was a hallowed site, as two great kings of Prussia, Frederick William I (1688-1740) and his son Frederick the Great (1712-86), lay buried there.

The ceremony was a magnificent one. The crown prince of Germany was there, with his wife, and so was the president of Germany, the aging Paul von Hindenburg, a man steeped in the country's old military traditions. He was proudly wearing his grandest uniform. The choir began with a great hymn of praise, 'Now Let Us All Thank God', which had been written to celebrate one of Frederick the Great's victories.

So this seemed to be a revival of Germany's past with its great military achievements; a celebration of a nation which had lived by God's law and been victorious as a result.

# The Rise of the Nazis

## CHARLES FREEMAN

HODDER
Wayland

an imprint of Hodder Children's Books

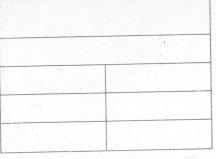

First published in 1997 by Wayland Publishers Ltd

This paperback edition published
in 2001 by Hodder Wayland,
an imprint of Hodder Children's Books

© Hodder Wayland 1997

This book was prepared for Wayland Publishers Ltd
by Ruth Nason.

Series editor: Alex Woolf
Series design: Stonecastle Graphics
Book design: LNbooks, Houghton Regis, Bedfordshire

British Library Cataloguing in Publication Data
Freeman, Charles
    The rise of the Nazis. – (New perspectives)
    1. Nationalsozialistische Deutsche Arbeiter-Partei – History
    – Juvenile literature 2. Germany – Politics and government
    – 1918-1933 – Juvenile literature 3. Germany – Politics and
    government – 1933-1945 – Juvenile literature
    I. Title
    943'.085

ISBN 0 7502 2600 5

Printed and bound in Italy by G. Canale & C.S.p.A., Turin

Cover photos: portrait of
Adolf Hitler, 1933, and
Nuremberg rally, 1933.

Page 1: a German cartoon
from 1932, depicting four
of the political parties that
were fighting each other in
the election: (left to right)
the Communists, the Nazis,
the Centre Party and the
Social Democrats.

## Acknowledgements

The Author and Publishers thank the following for their permission
to reproduce photographs: Camera Press: pages 6, 7, 26, 33b, 56;
Hulton-Getty Picture Collection: pages 4, 5, 9, 10, 16, 20, 21, 23, 24,
25, 27b, 29, 31, 33t, 36, 38, 44, 45, 48, 50, 57; John Frost Historical
Newspapers: pages 53, 54; Mary Evans Picture Library: cover, page
14; Popperfoto: pages 3, 15, 17r, 27t, 30, 37, 59; Topham Picturepoint:
pages 1, 8, 17l, 19, 32, 34, 39, 40, 42, 43, 46, 49, 51, 52, 55.

## A newspaper announcement, 21 March 1933

On the same day as the solemn opening of the Reichstag, a Munich newspaper included an announcement from Hitler's fellow Nazi leader and head of the SS (Schutzstaffel), Heinrich Himmler:

'On Wednesday, 22 March 1933, the first concentration camp will be opened near Dachau. It will accommodate 5,000 prisoners. Planning on such a scale we refuse to be influenced by any petty objection since we are convinced that this will reassure all those who have regard for the nation and serve their interests. Signed Heinrich Himmler, Acting Police-President of the City of Munich.'

Himmler went on to lay down the rules for the camp's inmates:

'The following offenders, considered as agitators, will be hanged: anyone who makes inciting speeches, and holds meetings, forms cliques, loiters about with others; who for the purpose of supplying the propaganda of the opposition with atrocity stories, collects true or false information about the concentration camps.' (Quoted in P. Johnson, *A History of the Modern World*)

But it was not all as it seemed. Walking beside the president, as he made his way up the aisle, was a man dressed more simply, in a frock coat. His military record had not been so distinguished: he had risen no higher than the rank of corporal and this in a war, the First World War, that Germany had lost less than fifteen years before. He was the new chancellor of Germany, an Austrian by birth, and leader of a political party, the National Socialists (Nazis), which had become the biggest in Germany. His name was Adolf Hitler and in his speech he promised that the past and the present would merge to create a new Germany, worthy of its proud history.

Each year, from 1927, the Nazi Party held a great rally at the ancient Bavarian city of Nuremberg. The rally was brilliantly organized to give an impression of order and of the massive power of the Nazi state. Above: the rally of 1936.

Two days later there was a different scene. It had none of the dignity of the ceremony in the Garrison Church. For its day-to-day business the Reichstag was to meet in the Kroll Opera House in Berlin. As the deputies (the elected members of the Reichstag) assembled, Hitler's supporters were out in force in the square outside. Those who were not from the Nazi Party were in for a rude awakening. Already members of the Communist Party had been prevented from attending at all. Now the other deputies found themselves insulted and jostled by men in Nazi uniforms.

Inside, the Opera House was decorated with great banners carrying the symbol of the Nazis, the swastika. Hitler's first business was to pass a law, the Enabling Law, which would allow him to govern without the consent of the Reichstag at all. He was actually calling on the Reichstag to sign its own death note. In an atmosphere heavy with intimidation he had his law passed within a day. No political party was able to offer him effective opposition.

### Speeches in the Reichstag, 23 March 1933

The only party to oppose the Nazis' Enabling Law was the Social Democratic Party. Its leader, Otto Wells, spoke as follows:

'We the German Social Democratic Party pledge ourselves solemnly in this historic hour to the principles of humanity and justice, of freedom and socialism. No enabling act can give you the power to destroy ideas which are eternal and indestructible.'

Hitler replied:

'You have come late, but yet you come! You are no longer needed ... The star of Germany will rise and yours will sink. Your death knell has sounded ... I do not want your votes. Germany will be free but not through you!' (Quoted in W. Shirer, *The Rise and Fall of the Third Reich*)

Germany had fallen under the control of the Nazi Party and it was not to be free of the party again until twelve years later. By then Germany lay in ruins after Hitler had led it to defeat in the Second World War. How was it possible for a country to fall under the domination of one man and one political party in this way?

Rubble and bombed-out buildings in Berlin at the end of the Second World War, July 1945.

# GERMANY IN DEFEAT, 1918-19

Even as late as the summer of 1918 most Germans had believed that Germany would win the First World War. Germany's main opponent in the east, Russia, had collapsed into revolution and withdrawn from the war. The Germans had seized vast areas of eastern Europe from Russia. On the Western Front, the British and French armies seemed to be in retreat. However, the German victories all proved hollow ones. By the autumn the British and French were fighting back, helped by enormous new resources of men and firepower from the USA, which had joined the war against Germany the year before. At the end of September 1918, the German generals suddenly realized that they had no more reserves and could no longer fight on. They called for an armistice, an end to the fighting.

As the fighting came to an end, Germany had to face up to the results of four years of fruitless warfare. Two million Germans had died and the country's economy was close to collapse. The shock of the sudden defeat was such that there was a new, intense hatred for all the authority figures who had brought Germany to its ruin. The Kaiser (the monarch) was forced to give up his throne. He fled to Holland and was never to return to his country. The German government, now headed by two formidable generals – Paul von Hindenburg and Erich Ludendorff, knew that it would have to hand over

Armed supporters of a workers' uprising against the new German government, 1919. The uprising was brutally crushed by the Freikorps, groups of ex-soldiers armed by the government, who freely massacred the workers.

power to civilians. But who would take over? Germany seemed awash with mutinous soldiers, striking workers and communists inspired by the recent revolution in Russia. It seemed as if order was breaking down completely.

The man who formed a new government was Friedrich Ebert, leader of the Social Democratic Party. This was a socialist party which had traditionally represented the German working classes. However, Ebert believed above all else in maintaining good order, and he was prepared to crush revolts by both workers and disaffected soldiers. He relied heavily on support from the army – and the generals, terrified of a revolution, were prepared to give it him. The German army, which had retreated in good order from the war front, was thus maintained in its traditional form.

To deal with unrest on the streets, Ebert used the Freikorps, gangs of ex-soldiers who were handed out uniforms and given the authority to keep order. In fact, they usually proved brutal and ill-disciplined in action and this encouraged other street armies to form to fight them. These 'street armies' were to become a permanent part of German political life until 1933.

By 1924 Germany had recovered some stability, partly due to the efforts of the president, Friedrich Ebert, who worked successfully with the army and police to keep order. Here Ebert inspects the police force on the fifth anniversary of the Weimar Republic, August 1924.

## THE MAIN POLITICAL PARTIES OF THE WEIMAR REPUBLIC

### The Social Democratic Party

This was the well-established party of the workers and had been powerful even before the First World War. It supported the Weimar Republic and provided the first Weimar president, Friedrich Ebert. Its views were moderate and it opposed disorder. It gradually lost votes to the Communist Party, which offered more revolutionary policies.

### The Communist Party

Founded in late 1918 in the chaos after the First World War. It was inspired by the Russian Revolution of 1917 and wished to overthrow the Weimar Republic, although it continued to contest elections. It was heavily involved in strikes and street disorder. It grew in size during the depression and offered the main threat to the Nazis. It saw the Social Democratic Party as its main rival for the workers' vote and its failure to stand beside the Social Democrats was one reason why Hitler was able to overthrow the Republic.

### The Centre Party

This party had been in existence before the First World War. It was originally a party for Catholics, half of whom voted for it. It had a broad range of support, from both conservatives and workers. It wished to preserve traditional values and protect the status of the Catholic Church. It maintained its support well but made no serious attempt to oppose Hitler in 1933 and was easily destroyed by him. In 1920 the more conservative Bavarian branch of the party broke off and its members sat separately as the Bavarian People's Party.

### The (German) National People's Party

This was founded after the First World War as a conservative party. Its main support was in rural areas. It wished for a return to the old Germany and the monarchy and was suspicious of new ideas and industrialization. Many of its members were sympathetic to Nazism and the party supported Hitler's Enabling Law in 1933.

There were also many smaller parties which were able to gain a foothold in the Reichstag through the system of proportional representation.

## The Weimar Constitution

One of Ebert's first tasks was to create a new democratic German constitution to replace the old discredited one, which had been dominated by the Kaiser, the landed classes and the generals. There were high hopes that this would be possible when, in an election in January 1919, the German voters turned their back on revolution. They voted for the traditional parties, among them Ebert's Social Democrats and the moderate Centre Party. All these parties agreed to work together to frame a new constitution. Fearing unrest in Berlin, their delegates met in the university town of Weimar and the constitution they drew up is known as the Weimar Constitution.

The Weimar Constitution aimed to give power to the people. Germany would now be a republic. Instead of a monarch there was to be a president, elected for seven years at a time by the voters as a whole. The president was given wide powers. He was commander of the armed forces, he appointed the chancellor (the senior government minister) and could call elections. If order broke down in Germany, the president could use the armed forces to take control. Normally, however, laws would be made by the Reichstag, the German parliament, which was given far more power than it had ever held before.

The members of the Reichstag were to be elected by the people as a whole but, in order to let all political opinions be heard, a

The shock of defeat in war left a strong anti-war feeling among many Germans. Here, in the 1920s, demonstrators from the Association of Friends of Religion and Peace Among Nations stand under a banner urging 'Thou shalt not kill'.

new system of election, known as proportional representation, was introduced. What this meant was that each political party drew up a list of candidates; then, for every 60,000 votes the party received, it could select one of these candidates as a Reichstag deputy. This was certainly democratic. The problem was that a host of smaller parties, with a few hundred thousand supporters, could gain a few members of parliament and no one party would have a majority in the Reichstag. Governments in the Weimar Republic were likely to be coalition governments in which a number of parties with different political ideas had to work together. This was to prove a major weakness.

## The Versailles Treaty

In May 1919 the new government was faced with a dreadful dilemma. The victors of the war, the Allies (the USA, Britain, France and Italy), who had been meeting in the great palace of Versailles near Paris, presented Germany with the terms of a peace treaty.

Under the Versailles Treaty, Germany lost land to France, Belgium, Denmark, Lithuania and Poland. West Prussia became a Polish 'corridor', splitting Germany in two.

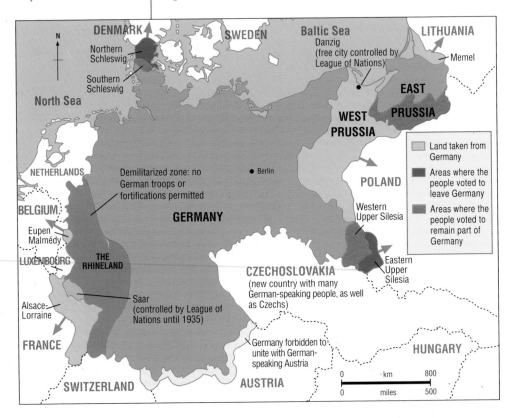

## The War Guilt Clause

Clause 231 of the Versailles Peace Treaty was particularly humiliating to the German government:

'The Allied and Associated Governments affirm and Germany accepts the responsibility of Germany and her allies for causing all the loss and damage to which the Allied and Associated Governments and their nationals have been subjected as a consequence of the war imposed upon them by the aggression of Germany and her Allies.'

There had been some hopes that the treaty would not be harsh. The US President Woodrow Wilson had promised that it would be fair, and many Germans thought that the Allies would be sympathetic to their new democratic government. They were horrified when they read the terms.

Germany and its allies, Austria-Hungary and Turkey, were to bear responsibility for causing the war and would have to pay compensation (later known as reparations) to the victors for their losses. Germany would lose the territory of Alsace-Lorraine on its western border to France, and it was not allowed to keep troops or fortifications in the Rhineland. The proud German army was in any case to be reduced to 100,000 men, no more than the size of a police force. Germany was not allowed to build an air force or navy. Particularly devastating was the loss of much of eastern Germany to Poland. A Polish 'corridor', designed to give Poland access to the sea, divided German territory into two, so that eastern Prussia was left isolated within Poland – 'a strip of flesh torn from our body,' as one German described it. Even the way the treaty was to be signed was humiliating. The German delegates to the peace conference were not allowed to discuss its terms and were told that the war would be resumed if they did not sign.

### Signing the peace treaty

Robert Lansing, Secretary of State to the US President Woodrow Wilson, described the German delegates as they signed the treaty:

'It was as if men were being called upon to sign their own death-warrants ... With pallid faces and trembling hands they wrote their names quickly and were then conducted back to their places.'
(From *The Peace Negotiations*)

Back in Germany there was shock. The government hesitated before signing, and the army spoke boldly of renewing the war. But soon all realized the hopelessness of Germany's position and, on 28 June 1919, the German delegates signed the treaty. For German nationalists there was only shame. There was talk of 'the November criminals', those civilians, it was said, who had made the undefeated German armies surrender in the first place. The Weimar Republic, which carried the hopes of a democratic and

Greed, Revenge and two other devils gloat over the Versailles Treaty in this German cartoon.

### Reactions of the German people

Anne Wittenberg grew up in Berlin in the 1920s. She remembers those days:

'Berlin was very political. By the time I was fourteen, we were profoundly aware of the gaps between rich and poor, between classes and castes. At the end of the school year during which we had studied the Versailles Treaty, we commemorated it with a mourning procession in the schoolyard. At the end of it, we solemnly tore up a copy of the treaty, threw it in a prepared garbage pail and set fire to it.' (Quoted in G. Sereny, *Albert Speer: His Battle with Truth*)

## 66 Reparations

The compensation that Germany was
required to pay for the First World War
was fixed at 132,000,000,000 gold marks
(£6,600,000,000). In 1921 a British
economist, J. M. Keynes, argued against
the policy:

'The policy of reducing Germany to
servitude for a generation, of degrading
the lives of millions of human beings,
and of depriving a whole nation of
happiness should be abhorrent and
detestable ... Some preach it in the name
of justice. In the great events of man's
history justice is not so simple.'
(From *The Economic Consequences
of the Peace*) 99

John Maynard Keynes,
1883-1946.

peaceful Germany, could not have had a worse start.
Many Germans, and the army in particular, felt no
commitment to democratic government if this
government was in charge.

## 66 A spirit of revenge

A historian, Anthony Wood, makes this comment on the peace treaty:

'The fundamental significance of Versailles was emotional rather than
rational. Allied statesmen, urged on by the pressure of public opinion,
had made peace in a spirit of revenge. The cries of 'Hang the Kaiser'
and 'squeezing the German lemon until the pips squeak' were
indicative of the desire not merely for a guarantee of future security,
but for the national humiliation of Germany ... The Germans saw
every difficulty in subsequent years as a further indignity that they
alone must suffer as a result of the hated Treaty of Versailles.'
(From *Europe 1815-1960*) 99

# THE YOUNG HITLER

Even before the terms of the Versailles Treaty were known, Germans had been shocked by the news of the armistice. One of them, an Austrian who had fought in the German armies, heard the news while he was in hospital recovering from having been temporarily blinded by a gas attack on the Western Front. His was a bitter reaction. 'I could stand it no more ...', he wrote later. 'While everything went black before my eyes, stumbling, I groped my way back to the dormitory, threw myself on the cot and buried my burning head in the covers and pillow. I had not wept since the day I had stood at the grave of my mother.' The twenty-nine-year-old Adolf Hitler vowed at that moment that he would seek out and destroy those people who he believed had been responsible for Germany's defeat.

Hitler as a soldier in the First World War, 1914-18. Hitler served throughout the war as an ordinary soldier and earned medals for bravery.

It seemed an extraordinary dream, but it was to become true – and in a way more horrific than anyone could have imagined. Adolf Hitler was to create a party, the Nazi Party, which, just fifteen years later, would seize power in Germany. He was to revive the shattered military strength of the country and lead it into a war, the Second World War (1939-45), in which Germany would overrun most of Europe. In the wake of the war millions of soldiers would die and millions more – Jews, gypsies, and other human beings whom the Nazis considered inferior – would be eliminated in extermination and labour camps. How could one man transform a nation into such a powerful and evil force?

## Hitler's background

Hitler's father was a customs official for the Austrian-Hungarian empire, on the empire's border with Germany. He was a cold and distant man, aged fifty-two and in his third marriage when Hitler was born in 1889. Hitler's mother was twenty-three years younger than her husband, a withdrawn woman who had suffered two still-births before the birth of Hitler and his sister. When Hitler's father died in 1903, there were only women in the home.

Something of the stern nature of Hitler's father, Alois, can be seen in the picture above. Hitler adored his mother, Klara (above left), and was devastated by her death in 1907.

## Hitler at school

In 1924, one of Hitler's teachers, Professor Eduard Humer, remembered:

'I can recall the gaunt, pale-faced youth pretty well. He had definite talent, though in a narrow field. But he lacked self-discipline, being notoriously quarrelsome, wilful, arrogant and irascible. He had obvious difficulty in fitting in at school. Moreover he was lazy; otherwise, with his gifts, he would have done very much better ... But his enthusiasm for hard work evaporated all too quickly. He reacted with ill-concealed hostility to advice or reproof; at the same time, he demanded of his fellow pupils their unqualified subservience, fancying himself in the role of leader.'
(Quoted in F. Jetzinger, *Hitler's Youth*)

## Hitler assesses the years in Vienna

'Vienna was and remained for me the hardest, though most thorough school of my life. I had set foot in this town while still half a boy and left it a man, grown and grave. In this period there took shape within me a world picture and a philosophy which became the granite foundation of all my acts. In addition to what I then created, I have had to learn little; and I have had to alter nothing.' (From *Mein Kampf*)

Hitler did poorly at school and had left for good by 1905. In 1907 he moved to Vienna, the capital of the Austrian-Hungarian empire, in the hopes of entering the Academy of Fine Arts. He was rejected then, and again in 1908.

In December 1907 his mother died painfully from cancer. Her slow death seems to have had a traumatic effect on Hitler. Her doctor said that he had never seen anyone so overwhelmed with grief.

Back in Vienna after this, Hitler was on his own, a lonely, insecure young man. He had a small income and earned a little more from painting, but he lived on the margins of the great bustling city, often in cheap lodging houses. He brooded deeply on the injustices he believed he had suffered. He needed a cause,

## An obsession with the Jews

'Since I had begun to concern myself with this question and become aware of the Jews, Vienna appeared to me in a different light than before. Wherever I went, I began to see Jews, and the more I saw the more sharply they became distinguished in my eyes from the rest of humanity. Particularly the inner city and the districts north of the Danube canal swarmed with a people which even outwardly had lost all resemblance to Germans ... Gradually I began to hate them.' (From *Mein Kampf*)

something to fight for, and a scapegoat, someone to blame. His cause became German nationalism, the belief that the German race – of which he, as an Austrian, was a member – was superior to others. His scapegoat was the Jews who, he believed, were undermining traditional German values.

Anti-Semitism (prejudice against Jews) was a powerful force across Europe. It was found in France, Russia and the Austrian-Hungarian empire and was no stronger in Germany than in those other countries. Its dark roots lay in the belief that Jews were responsible for the death of Christ. But, also, Jews had played a major part in the rapid industrialization of Europe and people who had been unsettled by such changes tended to blame the Jews for their insecurity. Hitler's own anti-Semitism gnawed away at him until it became an obsession. For him, Jews were behind every misfortune and were even linked to the spread of communism. Hitler was already dreaming that he would rid the world of both Jews and communists.

## Hitler moves to Germany and joins the army

In 1913 Hitler drifted across the border into the southern German state of Bavaria and went to live in the Bavarian capital, Munich. He was probably trying to escape military service in Austria and was no happier in Munich than in Vienna. But when war broke out in August 1914, he at last found a purpose in life. He was accepted as a volunteer for the German army and served as a courier, running between the trenches and the command posts further back.

Hitler returned to Bavaria after the First World War and, during the 1920s, tried hard to live like the natives. Here he is dressed in Bavarian national costume.

The start of the First World War was greeted with enthusiasm throughout Europe. Few realized the horror it would bring. Here, crowds in Munich greet the outbreak of war in August 1914. By chance, the cameraman captured Hitler rejoicing among them.

While never promoted beyond the rank of corporal, he was a good soldier and found, among his fellow soldiers, the comradeship that he had missed in Vienna and Munich. He even earned awards for bravery.

At the end of the war, fit again after the gas attack, he stayed in the army and in Germany. He was posted back to Munich. The army paid him to keep an eye on the revolutionary movements which were sweeping Germany after its defeat. His job was to make sure that soldiers did not join these movements. He was one among millions making their way in the harsh world of the shattered and demoralized Germany.

### Hitler as a soldier

Hitler's war record was good and he enjoyed the comradeship offered by the army. A colonel who knew him in the war wrote in 1922:

'Hitler set a shining example to those around him. His pluck and his exemplary bearing throughout each battle exerted a powerful influence on his comrades and this, combined with his admirable unpretentiousness, earned him the respect of superiors and equals alike.'
(Quoted in W. Maser, *Hitler*)

# THE BIRTH OF A MOVEMENT, 1919-24

After the First World War, a mass of small political parties emerged in Germany. One of these was the German Workers' Party, founded in Munich in January 1919. It was dedicated to the belief that workers should be loyal to Germany rather than to international communism, which had been given an enormous boost by the success of the Russian Revolution. It also contained a strong streak of anti-Semitism.

In September 1919 Hitler was sent by the army to report on the German Workers' Party. At this stage it was small and poorly organized, but Hitler was attracted by it and its ideas. Perhaps he sensed too that its tiny size would give him scope to dominate it. He was soon invited to join the party's committee, with responsibility for recruitment and propaganda. And then he discovered something surprising: that he had a genius for public speaking.

Germany's defeat in the First World War led to national humiliation and economic misery. This scene in Berlin, in June 1919, shows some of the despair that people felt.

At meeting after meeting in the beerhalls of Munich, he would pour out his obsessions: the appalling state of Germany after the peace treaty, the responsibility of the Jews and the communists for the disasters Germany had suffered, and the need for the German people, united with Germans living in eastern Europe

Although Germany was a unified nation, governed from Berlin, the different states retained a strong sense of local identity.

## Hitler and the German Workers' Party

Hitler described his first meeting with the committee of the German Workers' Party in 1919:

'The tavern in which the meeting was to take place was the Alte Rosenbad in the Herrenstrasse, a very run down place ... I went through the ill-lit dining room in which not a soul was sitting, opened the door to the back room, and there I was face to face with the Committee. In the dim light of a grimy gas lamp four young people sat at a table, among them the author of the little pamphlet who greeted me most joyfully and bade me welcome as a new member of the German Workers' Party.' (From *Mein Kampf*)

### The power of speech

Hitler wrote of the power of speech:

'The power which has always started the greatest religious and political avalanches in history rolling has from time immemorial been the magic power of the spoken word and that alone. The broad masses of the people can be moved only by the power of speech. All great movements are popular movements, volcanic eruptions of human passions and emotional sentiments, stirred either by the cruel goddess of distress or by the firebrand of the word hurled among the masses.' (From *Mein Kampf*)

– in Czechoslovakia, Austria and Poland – to find their voice as a single nation. Germany, he argued, had a right to expand east to find 'living room' (Lebensraum) for its people. These were Hitler's dreams, but he made them also into the dreams of his audiences, who were enthused by his oratory.

### Hitler's impact on an audience

One of Hitler's early supporters, Putzi Hanfstaengl, describes the impact of his speeches in the beerhalls of Munich:

'On this evening he was at his best. I looked round at the audience. Where was the nondescript crowd I had seen only an hour before? What was suddenly holding these people who, overwhelmed by inflation, were engaged in a struggle to keep themselves within the line of decency? The hubbub and the mug-clattering had stopped, and they were drinking in every word. Only a few yards away was a young woman, her eyes fastened on the speaker. Transfixed as though in some devotional ecstasy, she had ceased to be herself, and was completely under the spell of Hitler's despotic faith in Germany's future greatness.'

The SA uniform.
The SA were known as 'Brownshirts' in the same way as Mussolini's fighting force in Italy were known as 'Blackshirts'.

## The founding of the Nazi Party

In early March 1921 the German Workers' Party was renamed the National Socialist German Workers' Party or, more usually, the Nazi Party (from mixing letters from the German words 'National' and 'Sozialistische'). After a power struggle with the older members of the party Hitler emerged as its leader in July 1921. Leadership and domination of those around him had become essential to him. He seemed to have no real sympathy for the plight of his listeners, and was more interested in working them up, by his speeches, into a frenzy of enthusiasm for a rebuilt Germany under his leadership.

Hitler knew, too, that if he was to survive as leader, the party had to be disciplined and well organized. He adopted powerful symbols such as the swastika, an ancient symbol of 'good luck', which now appeared on banners and the armbands of party members. The colours of Germany's imperial flag were red, black and white and so a swastika was always drawn as black within a white circle on a red background.

In order to police meetings and defend party members, Hitler founded his own street army, the SA (Sturmabteilung) or Stormtroopers. The SA was

### The struggle

The Nazis believed that life was a struggle for superiority between different social and racial groups. Violence was never far below the surface. In a speech in Munich in November 1922, Hitler said:

'The communists taught – 'If you will not be my brother, I will bash your skull in'. Our motto will be – 'If you will not be a German I will bash your skull in'. For we are convinced that we cannot succeed without a struggle. We have to fight with ideas, but also, if necessary, with our fists.' (Quoted in A. Bullock, *Hitler: A Study in Tyranny*)

especially attractive to young ex-soldiers and members of the Freikorps. It had its own uniform, with a brown shirt, and behind its façade of army discipline it had no inhibitions about behaving violently towards its opponents. For his own personal bodyguard Hitler created a smaller, even tougher group, the SS (Schutzstaffel). With their grey coats and death's head cap badges, the SS were later to emerge as an instrument of terror.

Members of the Rotfront, the communist fighting force which battled with the SA.

SS men on parade.

Although the Nazis claimed to be a workers' party, most of their members now came from middle-class groups – craftsmen, minor civil servants and students – many of whom had wealthier backgrounds. They were drawn to the party by fear: fear that they would lose their jobs and middle-class respectability or fear that they would be overwhelmed by a communist revolution.

# The great inflation of 1923

In 1923 Germany underwent massive inflation, with the result that money lost its value. Those mostly middle-class Germans who had savings saw them disappear. Konrad Heiden was a German who lived through those times. He remembered:

'On Friday afternoons in 1923, long lines of manual and white collar workers waited outside the pay windows of the big German factories, department stores, banks, offices ... staring impatiently at the electric wall clock, slowly advancing until at last they reached the window and received a bag full of paper notes. According to the figures inscribed on them the paper notes amounted to seven hundred thousand, or five hundred million, or three hundred and eighty billion, or eighteen trillion marks – the figures rose from month to month, then from week to week, finally from day to day. With their bags the people moved quickly to the door, all in haste, the younger ones running. They dashed to the nearest food store, where a line had already formed. When you reached the store a pound of sugar might have been obtainable for two millions; but by the time you came to the counter, all you could get for two millions was half a pound.' (Quoted in T. Howarth, *Twentieth Century History*)

As money lost its value in the great inflation of 1923, many Germans were reduced to buying their food by barter. Here middle-class Germans are forced to exchange their family silver and a violin for a sack of flour.

By 1923 Germany was suffering acute unemployment and inflation, partly because of the heavy reparations payments but partly because of the enormous debts left from the First World War. Further humiliations had come when the French army occupied the Ruhr valley, the centre of German industry, in order to squeeze out more reparations. This all helped recruitment. In early 1922, the Nazi Party had 6,000 members. A further 35,000 joined by the end of that year and the SA alone numbered some 15,000. By 1923 the party membership totalled 55,000.

Top: Benito Mussolini (third from left), leader of the Italian Fascist Party, with his 'Blackshirts'. He seized power after his 'March on Rome' in 1922. Bottom: Munich, November 1923. Stormtroopers including Himmler (holding the flag) wait to hear the result of Hitler's coup. It was a humiliating failure.

## The beerhall coup

In 1923 the Nazi Party was still rooted in Bavaria. Bavaria was a conservative state with a proud military tradition, and its government was hostile to the Social Democratic national government in Berlin. It was this which made Hitler dream up a wild plan. Why not seize control of the Bavarian government and then force its leaders to join with the Nazis to march to Berlin to take over power in Germany? After all, in Italy, a young adventurer called Benito Mussolini, leader of the Fascist Party, which was very similar to Hitler's, had done the same with his 'March on Rome' in October 1922.

Hitler managed to persuade General Ludendorff, who had come to be seen as a German war hero, to join him. However, there was never much hope of success. The uprising, or coup, was set for 8 November and the plan was to

seize the members of the Bavarian state government while they were speaking in a beerhall and then persuade them to join the uprising. It was a fiasco. The Bavarian politicians were captured but then escaped. The police and the army remained loyal, and the next day, as 2,000 Nazis marched into the centre of Munich in a last hope of saving the coup, they were easily rounded up. Sixteen were killed and many others wounded. Ludendorff bravely marched to the end but Hitler, slightly injured, had already fled. He was arrested two days later.

## Appealing for support

Shortly before his arrest after the the failed coup of 8-9 November, Hitler appealed to his followers:

'Comrades! We stood in the field, shoulder to shoulder, of one mind. Nonetheless, upon orders of traitors, the state police drew their guns on Germany's leaders, Ludendorff and Hitler, and shot at the people's liberators ... I, Hitler, was wounded [in fact, Hitler damaged his shoulder when he fell to the ground]; Ludendorff, as if protected by God, remained unhurt. But twenty of our best men were dead, and about a hundred men, women and children injured. The opponents suffered no losses. Comrades! Do you wish to be part of the murderers or will you help to liberate Germany? You will not fight for treacherous Jews. Your German loyalty brings you to our side ...' (Quoted in G. Sereny, *Albert Speer: His Battle with Truth*)

Hitler and Ludendorff were put on trial for high treason. It could have been a humiliating experience, bringing an end to the Nazi movement. However, Hitler realized that his trial gave him a platform. He made a powerful and impassioned speech, saying that he was no more than a German patriot. How could he be called a traitor when he was only seeking to overthrow the traitors who had signed the Versailles Treaty? The court, terrified of being considered unpatriotic, gave him the minimum sentence of five

## History will judge

Hitler used the Munich court where he was tried for treason in March 1924 as a platform from which to speak to the German people:

'Gentlemen, judgment will not be passed on us by you; judgment will be passed on us by the eternal court of history ... Even if you find us guilty a thousand times over, the goddess of the eternal tribunal of history will smilingly tear apart the proposal of the prosecutor and the sentence of the court, because she will acquit us.'

years and acquitted Ludendorff completely. In fact, Hitler was only in prison for a few months and was released in December 1924.

## Mein Kampf

Hitler served his prison sentence in Landsberg, a fortress outside Munich. It was not a harsh existence: he could mix with other Nazis and, above all, he could write. It was now that he composed the story of his life and his dreams, *Mein Kampf* ('My Struggle'), the book which was to become the Bible of the Nazi movement.

Hitler spent several months of 1924 in Landsberg prison, together with other leading Nazis. Second from the right is Rudolf Hess, to whom Hitler dictated *Mein Kampf* and who later became his deputy.

*Mein Kampf* was such a badly organized and unreadable book that not many people bothered to study it. However, Hitler's ideas were spelled out in it for all to see. He poured out all his hatreds, for Jews and communists, and his dreams that a powerful Germany would earn a new place in Europe through conquest of its enemies. Underlying his ideas was an obsession with race. The Germans, he claimed, were members of a superior Aryan race which deserved its supremacy over lesser races, the Slavs of eastern Europe, Asians and blacks. Such thoughts fuelled his determination to revive the party once he was released.

# WILDERNESS YEARS, 1924-9

When Hitler was released from prison at the end of 1924, the Nazi Party seemed in ruins. Hitler had discredited himself with many respectable Germans by his attempt to seize power. He was forbidden to speak, for a time, in most states of Germany. Germany was also entering more settled times. New investment was entering the country, 20,000,000,000 dollars of it from the USA alone, so that by 1929 German industry was producing as much as it had done in 1913. Germany also began to build better relationships with its neighbours. The Foreign Minister Gustav Stresemann was an important figure here. He negotiated carefully to improve Germany's position with France and Italy and to ease the crushing reparations payments. The frustrations on which Hitler had built his movement seemed to be disappearing.

Gustav Stresemann, German chancellor and foreign minister, 1923-9. He was probably the only German politician with the ability to counter Hitler, but tragically he died of overwork in 1929.

## A change of tactics

In 1924, Hitler planned a new way of achieving power. He told Luedecke, who helped find funds for the Nazi Party in the 1920s:

'When I resume work it will be necessary to pursue a new policy. Instead of working to achieve power through an armed coup, we shall have to hold our noses and enter the Reichstag against the Catholic and Marxist [Communist] deputies. If out-voting them takes longer than out-shooting them, at least the result will be guaranteed by their own [Weimar] constitution. Any lawful process is slow ... Sooner or later we will have a majority – and after that, Germany.' (Quoted in K. Luedecke, *I Knew Hitler*)

Hitler, however, never lost his confidence that the party would triumph. He realized that his attempted coup had made people suspicious of him and the Nazis, and he concluded that it would now be more sensible to try to win seats in the Reichstag. He needed also to reach out beyond Bavaria to the rest of Germany. The problem lay in keeping an enlarged national party united under his leadership.

In the industrial north of Germany, there were local Nazi leaders, such as the brothers Gregor and Otto Strasser, who wanted to build a party of workers. While Hitler talked of the Nazi Party being a nationalist party (for all Germans), they talked of it as a socialist party (primarily for workers). They saw their enemies as the Communists and the Social Democrats and they talked of a workers' state of Germans, with Jews expelled. They felt that Hitler, who was after all an Austrian, was hardly the right kind of leader for such a movement.

It took all of Hitler's political skills to win back power for himself, and he was not firmly in control of the party until 1926. At the party conference that year, his followers saluted him as their leader with their arms stretched out towards him – the infamous Nazi salute, copied in fact from Mussolini's supporters in Italy.

## Goering and Goebbels

In these years Hitler also drew in two of his key supporters, Hermann Goering and Joseph Goebbels.

Intelligent, witty and larger than life, Goering had been a flamboyant air ace in the First World War. In 1922 he joined the Nazi Party and became the first leader of the SA, but then he left Germany after the failed beerhall coup in Munich. He returned in 1928 when Hitler asked him to become one of the party's members in the Reichstag.

Above: Gregor Strasser. Below: Three of the main Nazi leaders: Hermann Goering (left), Julius Streicher, editor of a viciously anti-Semitic newspaper, and Joseph Goebbels.

Goebbels, like many Germans of the time, was an unhappy, frustrated man. He was also deeply embarrassed by his club foot. He saw Hitler as a personal saviour. Like Hitler, he was a fine speaker and violently anti-Semitic. His real genius, however, was for propaganda. He brilliantly masterminded the Nazi political campaigns through the Nazi newspapers and later through the radio.

### Hero worship

In his diary in November 1925, Joseph Goebbels recorded:

'Hitler is there. Great joy. He greets me like an old friend. And looks after me. How I love him! What a fellow. Then he speaks. How small I am. He gives me his photograph. Heil Hitler. I want Hitler to be my friend. His photograph is on my desk.' (Quoted in J. Fest, *The Face of the Third Reich*)

Goebbels' quick mind and sharp tongue made him an ideal choice as propaganda minister when Hitler came to power.

### Party organization
In these 'wilderness years' after his release from prison, Hitler reorganized the Nazi Party to make it more effective nationally. Germany was divided into Gaue (districts), each under a Gauleiter who was directly responsible to Hitler and the small committee which ran the party with him. Goebbels was made Gauleiter in Berlin and took on the job of smashing up the large local Communist Party while ridiculing the local police chief at the same time. His aim was to break down order so that the Nazis could reap the benefit. Like Hitler, he cared less for Germany and the Germans than for his own personal power.

Alongside the destructive side of Nazism came the great party rallies. These presented the Nazis as a disciplined and patriotic movement whose only aim was a decent and respected Germany enjoying its rightful place in Europe. In 1927 the annual rally was held for the first time at the ancient city of Nuremberg. The rally was a theatrical spectacle, with the SA in massed ranks, rows of banners, great torchlight parades and a carefully staged build-up of enthusiasm to the moment when Hitler appeared to make a rousing speech. After this, with every year that passed, the Nuremberg rallies grew larger and more theatrical.

Above: Nazi supporters salute massed banners.
Below: Searchlights used at the 1938 Nuremberg rally.

The Hitler Youth movement catered for ten to eighteen year olds and any ambitious young German was expected to join. Uniforms, banners and oaths of loyalty were important.

 ## The arrival of Hitler

A new Nazi Party member described the arrival of Hitler at a meeting in 1926:

'A storm of jubilation rising from afar, from the street and moving into the lobby, announced the coming of the Führer [leader]. And then suddenly the auditorium went wild, as he strode resolutely in his raincoat and without a hat to the rostrum. When the speech came to an end, I could not see out of my eyes any more. There were tears in my eyes, my throat was all tight from crying. A liberating scream of the purest enthusiasm discharged the unbearable tension as the auditorium rocked with applause. I looked around discreetly, and noticed that others, too, men and women and young fellows, were as deeply affected as I ... There were people around me who felt the same as I, who were looking at each other in joyful rapture, as if they were all one family or a brotherhood or a new firm and happy community where everyone could read in the other's eyes a solemn oath of loyalty.'
(Quoted in P. Merkl, *Political Violence under the Swastika*)

# A Nazi meeting

A police report on a Nazi meeting on 9 March 1927 recorded:

'It is now half past eight. From the entrance come roars of Heil. Brownshirts [the SA] march in, the band play, the crowd cheers noisily. Hitler appears in a brown raincoat, walks swiftly, accompanied by his retinue, the whole length of the stadium and up to the stage. The crowd gesticulate in happy excitement, wave, continually shout Heil, stand on the benches, stamp their feet thunderously. Then comes a trumpet blast. Sudden silence.

'Amid roars of welcome from the spectators, the Brownshirts now march into the hall in rank and file, led by two rows of drummers and then the flag. The men salute in the manner of the [Italian] Fascists, with outstretched arms. The audience cheers them. On the stage Hitler has similarly stretched out his arm in salute. The music surges up. Flags move past, glittering standards with swastikas inside the wreath and eagles, modeled on the ancient Roman military standards. Perhaps two hundred men file past. They fill the arena and stand at attention while the flag-bearers and the standard-bearers people the stage ...

'Hitler steps swiftly to the front of the stage. He speaks without a manuscript, at first in a slow, emphatic way; later the words come tumbling forth ... He gesticulates with arms and hands, jumps agitatedly about and is bent on fascinating the thousands in the audience, who listen with close attention ...' (Quoted in J. Fest, *Hitler*)

## The 1928 election

The real test of success, however, was whether the party could win votes. In 1928 an election was due. Germany was now prosperous and stable. The reparations payments were being reduced and people were tending to forget the humiliations of the war. To the Nazis' dismay, they were decisively rejected by the electorate. The Nazi Party won only 2.6 per cent of the votes, a total of twelve seats out of over 600. Four years after his release from prison, Hitler was no nearer to his dream of power.

# THE NAZIS' DRIVE TO POWER, 1929-32

In 1929 came the Stock Market Crash in New York, and a great depression in world trade followed. Germany was hit particularly hard because so much American money had been invested in the country and this was now withdrawn. The numbers of German unemployed soared. There were a million in October 1929, three million in September 1930, and over five million two years later. The blow of the depression was all the more crushing because so many gains had been made in the previous five years. Now these gains seemed all to be swept away. The old contempt for the Weimar Republic revived. It seemed that parliamentary government had brought only a mass of small parties bickering with each other, none of them able to solve Germany's economic problems. No wonder that the idea of parliamentary democracy was discredited.

It was now that Hitler's hard work and confidence paid off. He hammered away at his basic beliefs with new enthusiasm. Once again he called for the rejection of the Versailles Peace Treaty and of reparations, an end to the influence of Jewish people, and the replacement of democracy by a strong government dedicated to the revival of German pride. Hitler was particularly clever to avoid spelling out a detailed programme. He made vague promises to everyone: to workers, that a revived Germany would give them jobs; to the middle class, that they

Hitler speaking in a Munich beerhall in the early 1930s. Hitler's ability to sell his message to a wide variety of audiences was one of his greatest political talents. Note Joseph Goebbels and Hermann Goering, both clapping, in the front row.

would have stability; to smaller farmers – who had flocked to the party in large numbers – that their pride in the land would be respected.

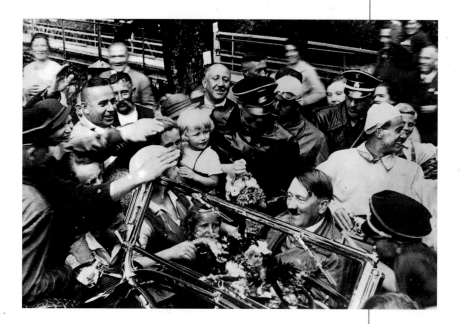

By 1930 Hitler was becoming a celebrity. Here crowds surround his car and shower him with flowers. Note the uniformed SS men protecting him.

For the young, he presented a new modern Germany in which technology would bring not just jobs but achievement, new roads, new factories, and – though this could only be hinted at – new weapons for the army. He showed the way by using an aeroplane for his campaigning. For older Germans, he harked back to traditional German values of the family and hard work. For businessmen, he would put on a suit and talk quietly of the need to deal with communists and unruly trade unions.

As a result, the Nazi Party now built up its membership from across the population, and it began to receive money from businessmen who valued its stand against communists. The party attracted civil servants, small farmers, ambitious students, and the unemployed. Traditionally, the National People's Party had won the votes of conservatives, especially in rural areas, but now these people began to turn instead to the Nazis. The National People's Party vote dropped by half between 1928 and 1930.

## ❝ The appeal of Nazism

Albert Speer became Hitler's chief architect in 1934. In his memoirs, *Inside the Third Reich,* he explains why Nazism attracted him in 1931:

'Here it seemed to me was hope. Here were new ideals, a new understanding, new tasks ... The perils of Communism which seemed inexorably on the way could be checked, Hitler persuaded us, and instead of hopeless unemployment, Germany could move towards economic recovery. He had mentioned the Jewish problem only in passing. But such remarks did not worry me, although I was not anti-Jewish; rather I had Jewish friends from my school days, like virtually everyone else. It must have been during these months that my mother saw an S.A. parade in the streets of Heidelberg. The sight of discipline in a time of chaos, the impression of energy in an atmosphere of universal hopelessness, seems to have won her over also.' ❞

A typical Nazi meeting was a blaze of colour, energy and disciplined good order which gave the sense of an irresistible power sweeping all before it. Music was used effectively. When an SA leader, Horst Wessel, was killed by a communist in Berlin in 1930, a patriotic song he had written, 'Raise High the Flag', was set to an old folk tune and became the stirring anthem of the Nazi Party, challenging even the German national anthem. At street level, however, the SA delighted in beating up its opponents, attacking the Communist Party which was itself attracting many new members.

Shot by communists in a dispute over a girl, Horst Wessel was cunningly transformed by Goebbels into a Nazi martyr and given an elaborate funeral.

The SA parade in front of Hitler, in Munich, 1932.

 ## A teacher hears Hitler speak

Frau Luise Solmitz, a Hamburg school teacher, attended a Nazi Party rally in 1932. She wrote in her diary:

'The April sun shone hot like in summer and turned everything into a picture of expectation. There is immaculate order and discipline ... Aeroplanes above us. Testing of the loudspeakers, buzzing of the cine cameras. It was nearly 3 pm. "The Führer is coming!" A ripple went through the crowds. Around the speakers' platform one could see hands raised in the Hitler salute. A speaker opened the meeting, nobody listened to him. A second speaker welcomed Hitler and made way for the man who had drawn 120,000 people of all classes and ages. There stood Hitler in a simple black coat and looked over the crowd, waiting – a forest of swastika pennants swished up, the jubilation of the moment was given vent in a roaring salute. His main theme – out of parties shall grow a nation, the German nation. He laid into the system – "I want to know what there is left to be ruined in this state!" When the speech was over, there was roaring enthusiasm and applause ...'

The Reichstag after the 1930 election. The Nazis sat together, their uniforms in marked contrast to the sober suits of the other members.

## Gaining votes

In the election of September 1930, the Nazi Party enjoyed an astonishing success. It attracted six and a half million voters, seven times the number in 1928. With 107 seats in the Reichstag it had become the second biggest party in Germany. (The Social Democrats, the traditional German workers' party, remained the biggest, although its support was falling.)

The Nazis had now won mass support in the rural areas of northern Germany, where many small farmers had suffered heavily in the depression. In the cities, the Nazis were stronger among the middle classes than they were among workers. The Communist Party was winning workers' votes from the Social Democratic Party, growing from 54 seats in the Reichstag in 1928 to 77 seats in 1930. But it was just this threat of growing communism that the Nazis were able to exploit in their propaganda. The Communists, the Nazis said, were in league with 'that Slav nation', Russia, and could only bring revolution and disorder. The Nazis, on the other hand,

## Nazis in the Reichstag, 1930

Toni Seiler, a Social Democratic Party member of the Reichstag commented on the Nazi members of the parliament in 1930:

'This was the elite of the 'Aryan' race – this noisy, shouting uniformed gang. I looked at their faces carefully. The more I studied them the more I was terrified by what I saw, so many men with the faces of criminals and degenerates. What a degradation to sit in the same place with such a gang.' (Quoted in J. Toland, *Hitler*)

spoke for Germany and order. When violent SA activities were reported in the press, the Nazis explained them away as the result of the SA's praiseworthy enthusiasm to save the German nation from its enemies.

## VOTING PATTERNS IN THE WEIMAR REPUBLIC

| Parties | Percentage of total votes cast in elections | | | | | | |
|---|---|---|---|---|---|---|---|
| | 1920 June | 1924 Dec. | 1928 May | 1930 Sept. | 1932 July | 1932 Nov. | 1933 March |
| Communist | 2.1 | 9.0 | 10.6 | 13.1 | 14.5 | 16.9 | 12.3 |
| Social Democratic | 21.7 | 26.0 | 29.8 | 24.5 | 21.6 | 20.4 | 18.3 |
| Centre | 13.6 | 13.6 | 12.1 | 11.8 | 12.5 | 11.9 | 11.2 |
| National People's | 15.1 | 20.5 | 14.2 | 7.0 | 6.2 | 8.9 | 8.0 |
| Nazis | — | 3.0 | 2.6 | 18.3 | 37.4 | 33.1 | 43.9 |

Through 1931 and 1932 the economic situation worsened. In 1932, Germany's industrial production was only half of that in 1928-9 and hundreds of banks had collapsed. The governments (made up of centre parties with Social Democratic Party support) muddled on without success, and disillusion with parliamentary government increased by the day.

## A newspaper interview

Hitler summed up his views in an interview with the *Leipziger Neueste* (Leipzig News) on 4 May 1931:

'They call me a stateless corporal and a housepainter. Is there anything improper in having earned one's daily bread by manual labour? ... The day of reckoning is not far off. An increasing number of industrialists, financiers, intellectuals and army officers are now looking for a man who will at last bring some order into affairs at home, who will draw the farmers, the workers and the officials into the German community once more.'
(Quoted in K. Fischer, *Nazi Germany*)

Posters for Hindenburg (above) and Hitler (below), in the presidential election of 1932. 'We want work and bread. Choose Hitler' was Hitler's slogan.

Hitler kept up the momentum of the Nazi movement. In April 1932 a new German president was to be elected. The first president of the Weimar Republic, Friedrich Ebert, had died in 1925 and been succeeded by the old German warlord, General von Hindenburg. Hindenburg stood again in the 1932 presidential election and won, with over nineteen million votes. But Hitler, who had now become a German citizen, stood against him and won over thirteen million votes.

## Hitler is close to power

In elections in July 1932, the Nazis emerged as the biggest party in the Reichstag, with some 230 seats. Hitler demanded that President Hindenburg appoint him as chancellor, the senior government minister, but Hindenburg refused. He had no time for Hitler, whom he considered an upstart, and let this be publicly known. His choice for chancellor was a conservative aristocrat, Franz von Papen, from the Centre Party.

Hitler seemed trapped and in yet another set of elections, in November 1932, the Nazis actually lost two million votes. The public were increasingly aware of the brutality of the SA, and Hitler's own popularity was damaged when he defended a gang of SA members who had murdered a communist in cold blood. Many believed that the Nazis had peaked. Donations fell off and the party faced a financial crisis.

 **Blood must flow**

A Nazi Stormtrooper song from the 1930s went:

'Blood must flow. Blood must flow!
Blood must flow as cudgel thick as hail!
Let's smash it up. Let's smash it up
That god-damned Jewish Republic.'

Yet Hitler in fact was very close to power. Von Papen had no real support in the country and was faced by the massed opposition of Nazis and Communists in the Reichstag. (The Communists increased their vote in the November 1932 elections and held 100 seats.)

Above left: a Communist demonstration in Berlin, July 1932.
Above: 'Are <u>these</u> people to rule you?' asked an anti-Nazi poster.

## Nazis versus communists

Street violence in Berlin centred on clashes between Nazis and communists. Arthur Koestler, a Hungarian-born journalist who was active in the European communist movement until the late 1930s, recalled:

'During that long hot stifling summer of 1932 we [the communists] fought our ding-dong battles with the Nazis. Hardly a day passed without one or two dead in Berlin. The main battlefields were the Bierstuben, the smoky little taverns of the working-class districts. Some of these served as meeting places for the Nazis, some as meeting places for us. To enter the wrong pub was to venture into the enemy lines. From time to time the Nazis would shoot up one of our meeting places. It was done in the classic Chicago tradition, a gang of SA men would drive slowly past the tavern, firing through the glass-panes, then vanish at break-neck speed.'
(From *The God that Failed*)

## A view of parliamentary government

Many Germans were disillusioned by the squabbling between different political parties. At the end of 1932, after two elections, one man observed:

'National Socialism was a revulsion by my friends against parliamentary politics, parliamentary debate, parliamentary government – against all the higgling and haggling of the parties, their coalitions, their confusions, and their connivings. It was ... the common man's repudiation of "the rascals". Its cry was "Throw them all out."' (Quoted in Milton Mayer, *They Thought They Were Free*)

Franz von Papen (above), a Catholic aristocrat, completely misjudged events, believing that he could control Hitler if he brought him into government.

Von Papen resigned as chancellor in December and was replaced by General von Schleicher. Von Schleicher fared no better and then von Papen hatched a new plan. In order to isolate the Communist Party, he persuaded Hindenburg to appoint Hitler as chancellor with himself, von Papen, as vice-chancellor. It would be better, he told Hindenburg, to bring Hitler into the government and control him, than to leave the Nazis outside as a dangerous force threatening the stability of the state. Hindenburg, by now an old and tired man, agreed. On 30 January 1933, Hitler, the leader of the biggest party in the Reichstag, was appointed chancellor.

1933. President Hindenburg sits alongside Hitler, now chancellor of Germany.

# THE NAZIS SEIZE POWER, 1933-4

Hitler's appointment as chancellor in January 1933 made little stir abroad. There were only two other Nazis among the government ministers: the Minister for the Interior, Wilhelm Frick, and Hermann Goering as a minister without any special responsibility. Most power still rested with President Hindenburg, who disliked Hitler. Von Papen believed that he had got Hitler boxed in. It was a fatal mistake.

Leading Nazis on the day after Hitler was made chancellor of Germany. Wilhelm Frick is seated. Goering stands on Hitler's left, and Ernst Roehm, the leader of the SA, is behind them. On the far right is Heinrich Himmler, head of the SS, who took responsibility for the first concentration camps.

Von Papen had no idea of Hitler's determination. He did not realize how cunning he was as a politician, nor how much energy there was in the Nazi Party. Even though the Nazis did not have much power, they behaved from the start as if they did. On the night of Hitler's appointment, a great parade of Nazis took place in Berlin. There was talk of a National Awakening, a new beginning for Germany.

## Celebrating Hitler's appointment

Goebbels recorded events in Berlin on the night that Hitler had been appointed chancellor:

'It is almost like a dream. The Führer is already working in the Chancellery. We are standing at the windows up there and watch as hundreds of thousands upon hundreds of thousands stream by their ancient President and young Chancellor and by the light of thousands of torches, cheer and sing their gratitude ... The new Reich is born ... victory after a struggle of fourteen years ... we have reached our goal. The German revolution begins.' (From *The Goebbels Diaries*)

February 1933. Hitler and Roehm meet with the SA to inspire their efforts in the Nazi election campaign. The SA took a leading role in disrupting the meetings of other parties.

Hitler worked fast. He announced at once that there would be a new election, in March. By February, he was meeting secretly with the army generals. The generals, most of whom came from old landed families with honourable military traditions, were still suspicious of Hitler, this Austrian corporal. They were contemptuous of the SA, seeing the Stormtroopers as just playing at being soldiers. However, they had never

been prepared to accept the Weimar Republic and Hitler told them what they wanted to hear: that there would be an honoured place for the army in the new Germany and that the restrictions of the Versailles Treaty would be thrown aside. They could plan, secretly, to rearm. Given such promises, the generals would certainly not oppose him.

### The Reichstag fire

Now the Nazis began to deal with their opponents. Goering was appointed Minister for the Interior in Prussia, the largest state in Germany, and set to work on bringing the police there under Nazi control. The SA were allowed to help the police keep order.

### Herman Goering, Chief of the Prussian Police

As Minister for the Interior in Prussia, Goering was in direct charge of the largest police force in Germany. He was exuberant in his new role. The comments he passed on many occasions reveal how unrestrained the Nazis were in the use of violence against their opponents.

On arriving on the scene of the Reichstag fire, 27 February 1933, he said: 'This is the beginning of the Communist revolution! We must not wait a minute. We will show no mercy. Every Communist official must be shot, where he is found. Every Communist deputy must this very night be strung up.'

In February 1933, after taking over the police: 'Every bullet that now leaves the mouth of a police pistol is my bullet. If you call that murder, then I am the murderer, for I gave the order and I stand by it.'

In May 1933: 'For us the people are divided into two parts: one which professes faith in the nation, the other who wants to poison and destroy. The police are not there to protect rogues, vagabonds, usurers and traitors. If people say that here and there someone has been taken away and maltreated, I can only reply, "You can't make omelettes without breaking eggs" ... even if we make a lot of mistakes, we shall at least act and keep our nerve. I'd rather shoot a few times too short or too wide, but at least I shoot.'

Communists were targeted as enemies of the state and they could now be beaten up openly. For the first time Jews were also being publicly humiliated.

The Nazi campaign against the Communist Party was given a boost on 27 February 1933 when the Reichstag building was burned down. A Dutch communist, Marinus van der Lubbe, was found by the fire and confessed to having started it, although suspicion remains that the Nazis had actually set fire to the building themselves. The very next day Hindenburg was persuaded to sign an emergency decree giving the government absolute control over meetings and newspapers and the power to arrest almost anyone they wanted.

### The election of March 1933

The election of 5 March took place in mounting hysteria. Goebbels was now in charge of the state radio and came into his own, shouting abuse at the Nazis' opponents. However, despite massive intimidation by the Nazis, Hitler still failed to reach a majority. The Nazis won 288 seats (44 per cent of the votes), but the Social Democrats and Communists still won 201 seats between them and the Centre Party another 73. If Hitler was to have a majority in the Reichstag he would have to rely on the support of the National People's Party, which had won 52 seats.

By the time of the first working session of the Reichstag on 23 March, the Nazis had done their work. Most of the Communist members had been arrested, and none of the rest dared to turn up. Also more than a sixth of the 120 Social Democrats failed to arrive. It was on this day that Hitler presented

27 February 1933. The Reichstag building goes up in flames. To this day no one is really sure who started the fire, but a young communist was arrested near the blaze and this gave the Nazis an excuse for dealing with the Communist Party.

## A decree of 14 July 1933

This decree made Germany a one-party state:

'The National Socialist German Workers' Party constitutes the only political party in Germany. Whoever undertakes to maintain the organizational structure of another political party or to form a new political party will be punished with penal servitude for up to three years or with imprisonment of from six months to three years.'

A year earlier, Hitler had said: 'I tell all these sorry politicians, "Germany will become one single party, the party of a great, heroic nation."'

the Reichstag with the Enabling Law, which would allow the government to rule in 'this state of emergency' without the Reichstag for the next four years. The National People's Party agreed to support the law. The Centre Party was tricked into supporting it with a number of meaningless promises. Only 94 Social Democrats were there to vote against it – not enough to prevent it being passed. From this time, the Reichstag met only when Hitler needed to harangue its members or announce important foreign policy decisions. In this way, parliamentary government, which Hitler had always hated, was quickly brought to an end.

## Ending opposition

Hitler now began to move his supporters into the government. Joseph Goebbels became a horribly effective minister of propaganda and Goering emerged as the most powerful man in Prussia. Over the next few months, other political parties were closed down so that, by July 1933, the Nazi Party was the only party allowed.

Joseph Goebbels harangues the masses. Goebbels was totally unscrupulous in the way he twisted facts to suit the Nazis' needs.

## Humiliating the Jews

One of the first moves of the Nazis on coming to power was to set in motion their anti-Jewish programme. This programme was checked when it appeared that it might threaten Hitler's relationship with his European neighbours, but it returned with a new horror and intensity in the late 1930s.

These are extracts from Goebbels' diaries for 1933:

'March 26. We are going to organize a radical boycott of all Jewish-owned shops in Germany.'

'March 28, 29, 30, 31. Today we announced the boycott: panic among the Jews ... approval from all members of government ... The boycott is fully organized. We press a button and it starts ... It will initially last one day; if the propaganda abroad ceases, we stop it; if not there will be no mercy ...

'April 1. Boycott fully effective in Berlin and the whole Reich. I drove through the business district to see for myself how it was working. All Jewish shops are closed, each guarded by the SA. The people support us with exemplary discipline. An imposing spectacle ... a huge moral victory for Germany: we have shown to everyone abroad that we can call on the whole nation for action without the least excesses. Once again the Führer has found the right solution.'

April 1933. The boycott of Jewish businesses was enforced by members of the SA who intimidated anyone wanting to enter Jewish shops.

The trade unions, already weakened by years of unemployment, were banned and replaced with a German Labour Front under Nazi control. In late 1933 and early 1934, the rights remaining to the German state governments, such as those of Prussia and Bavaria, were abolished. This was now a government ruled from Berlin and, in effect, under the control of one man, Adolf Hitler.

At street level the SA were exultant. They were now intent on their own revolution. They knew that no one could stop their rowdy and brutal behaviour. They beat up Jews and communists, smashed up the offices of trade unions, and humiliated passers-by.

On 1 April, with the help of Goebbels, they organized a boycott of Jewish businesses. The government gave them its support in a law of 7 April, which removed Jews and other suspected opponents of the Nazis from the civil service.

By May 1933 repression of free speech by the Nazis was the order of the day. Here books believed to offend German pride are being burned.

# The SA plots 'the second revolution'

Ernst Roehm made no secret of his disillusionment with Hitler as he saw him moving closer to the German army:

'Adolf is a swine. He will give us all away. He's getting matey with the generals – they are his cronies now ... the generals are a lot of old fogeys. They've never had a new idea ... I'm the nucleus of a new army, don't you see that? Don't you understand that what's coming must be new, fresh and unused? You only get the opportunity once to make something new and big that will help us lift the world off its hinges.' (Quoted in G. Craig, *Germany, 1866-1945*)

To boost their public image the Nazis ran Christmas charity concerts. This one, in 1933, was attended by leading Nazis and also minor aristocrats, such as Prince Eitel Frederick of Prussia, third from the left, who gave the Nazi Party some respectability among traditional Germans.

## Crushing the SA

The problem that remained was what role the SA was to play in the new state. Hitler was a good enough politician to know that, to survive, he needed to win and keep the support of middle-class Germans, especially those in the civil service and the army. Already many such people were joining the Nazi Party but, as law-abiding citizens, they could not help noticing and being offended by the antics of the SA. The SA now numbered over a million. Under their new commander, a swashbuckling ex-soldier by the name of Ernst Roehm, they talked openly of a second revolution in which they would be given jobs and perhaps even form 'a people's army' in the new state. After all, many of them had joined the SA simply because they were unemployed.

This talk frightened many: the army, those who desperately wished to avoid yet more upheavals, and also many leading Nazis, such as Goering, who were building up their own

police forces. Goering, in fact, was developing his own secret police known as the Gestapo, which would soon spread throughout Germany and become a symbol of terror for all who opposed the Nazis. The SA would upset these plans.

Goering and others fed stories to Hitler about Roehm's untrustworthiness and disloyalty. Hitler also heard from the army generals that they would have no regrets if the SA was dealt with. On 30 June 1934, after many hesitations, Hitler acted. He accused the SA of attempting a revolution and used the SS, originally a small bodyguard but now a brutal killing force, to do the dirty work. Roehm and other SA leaders were killed on what became known as 'the Night of the Long Knives'.

The British *Daily Express* for 2 July 1934 details the events of the Night of the Long Knives. The brutality of the regime was now clearly revealed to all those ready to face up to it.

## The army supports the Night of the Long Knives

In July 1934, General von Blomberg, the defence minister, declared:

'The Führer with soldierly decision and exemplary courage has himself attacked and crushed the traitors and murderers. The Army as the bearer of arms of the entire people, far removed from the conflicts of domestic politics, will show its gratitude through devotion and loyalty.'

Blomberg's view was that the army was the guardian of the German nation. It stood above (was 'far removed from') everyday politics and so had done nothing to protect the Weimar Republic.

A British newspaper marks the moment when Hindenburg dies and Hitler assumes power. Hindenburg was buried in a magnificent ceremony at Tannenberg, where he had won a notable victory in 1914 over invading Russian troops. The funeral ceremony helped cement Hitler's relationship with the army who were delighted that their general had received such honour. The army chiefs now accepted Hitler as their new supreme commander.

The Mexican artist Diego Rivera had no illusions about the Nazi regime, as his painting opposite, from 1933, shows.

The army was pleased and the officers made no complaints when, following the death of the aged President Hindenburg on 2 August 1934, Hitler took over his powers and declared himself Führer, leader of the nation and commander-in-chief of its army. The failed art student from Vienna had become absolute leader of Germany.

## Oath of loyalty

In 1934, German soldiers were required to swear this oath of loyalty to Hitler as commander-in-chief of the German armed forces:

'I swear by God this sacred oath, that I will yield unconditional obedience to the Führer of the German Reich and Volk, Adolf Hitler, the Supreme Commander of the Wehrmacht (army), and, as a brave soldier, will be ready at any time to lay down my life for this oath.'

Soldiers who were not Nazis were now bound to Hitler personally by this oath.

# CONCLUSION

In 1945, twelve years after he had seized power, Hitler and a few loyal supporters were sheltering underground in Berlin. Russian shells were pounding the city. The armies of Britain and the USA were crossing into Germany from the west. Hitler's great new Germany was in ruins. As the Allies reconquered Europe they uncovered concentration and extermination camps. The true horror of Nazism was exposed for everyone to see.

As Hitler's world crumbled, he wrote out a last statement: the German people had betrayed him. He

The Second World War began in September 1939, after Hitler invaded Poland. Here victorious German soldiers march into Poland.

had been right all along – they, his people, had not been good enough for him. It was, of course, Hitler who had done the betraying. He had led the German nation into defeat and left it in a state of destruction far worse, and with a burden of guilt far heavier, than it had experienced after the First World War.

Historians have argued about Hitler and the Germans ever since. Was there something in the German nation that made it welcome abusive leaders like Hitler? Or was the Weimar Republic doomed to failure? Certainly its signing of the harsh and humiliating Versailles Treaty damned it in the eyes of many and it never provided strong government, especially at times of crisis. Did the German people themselves betray

Defeat. Disillusioned Germans start clearing the rubble of the city of Dresden, which was bombed to pieces by Allied forces in 1945. This was the bitter aftermath of Nazism for the German people, as their own defeat brought home what others had suffered at their hands.

democracy? Certainly, if Hitler's opponents – the Social Democrats and the Communists, for instance – had united, they might have been able to prevent his rise. After all, Hitler never achieved a majority at an election, even in March 1933. Again, all too many Germans, including the army, turned a blind eye to the public violence of the Nazis and stood by while democracy was dismantled. Underlying these weaknesses, however, was the massive disillusion and despair caused by defeat in war, and then – just when hope seemed to be returning – by the shock of the great depression. It was the genius of Hitler to be able to sense this despair and transform it into a movement which seemed to offer hope and renewal. In fact, it brought only another experience of defeat and destruction for Germany.

 **Hitler and the German people**

William Carr summed up Hitler's effect on the German people in his book *Hitler, A Study in Personality and Politics*:

'What was compelling about Hitler and what distinguished his party from other right wing parties were not only the external trappings – the feverish activity, the endless marching, the mass rallies and the ceaseless propaganda drives – important though these were in gathering votes, but above all the ruthless will to victory and the fanatical sense of commitment emanating from the Führer and his followers. When Hitler promised to sweep out 'the old gang' he carried conviction. The old established middle class, frightened by the radicalisation of working class politics implied in the mounting Communist vote, felt instinctively that this man meant what he said: he would destroy Marxism [communism] and restore the old values.'

## The personality of Hitler

E. J. Feuchtwanger, in *From Weimar to Hitler, Germany, 1918-33*, concludes:

'Until the final years of the Weimar Republic there was little reason to suppose that the diverse and ill-assorted 'national' opposition could be formed into a battering ram to destroy the Republic. It needed the extreme pressure of the great depression, following so rapidly upon the previous crisis, to marshal these diverse forces and ideas behind National Socialism and Hitler. The personality of the Führer became a significant historical factor. Without his combination of demagogic gifts and political instinct the unified battering ram could hardly have come into operation. Luck was also with him because all the other players in the field turned out to be so inadequate and mistaken in their judgments.'

Clearing up. This time it is Nazi books that are being burned. Young Germans were faced with building a new democratic Germany out of the ruins of the old.

# DATE LIST

**1889**
**20 April**    Adolf Hitler is born in Austria.

**1914**
**August**      Outbreak of First World War. Hitler, now living in Munich, enlists in the German army.

**1918**
**November**    Germany surrenders. The First World War is over.

**1919**        A new constitution for Germany is drawn up at Weimar.
**June**        Germany signs the Treaty of Versailles.
**September**   Hitler's first meeting with the German Workers' Party. He soon joins the committee.

**1921**
**March**       The German Workers' Party is renamed the Nazi Party.
**July**        Hitler emerges as its leader.

**1923**        Germany is hit by inflation and its currency system collapses. The Nazis benefit from the economic chaos.
**November**    Hitler tries to seize power in Munich: the 'beerhall coup'. His uprising is easily defeated.

**1924**
**March –**
**December**    Convicted for his part in the coup, Hitler is imprisoned in Landsberg fortress. Here he writes *Mein Kampf*.

**1925-6**      Hitler regains control of the Nazi Party and focuses on winning seats in the Reichstag. Germany returns to political and economic stability.

**1928**
**May**         The Nazis win only 2.6 per cent of the votes, 12 seats, in the elections for the Reichstag.

**1929**
**October**     After further years of stability, the Stock Market Crash in New York leads to the great depression (1929-32). Unemployment in Germany soars.

**1930**
**September**   In elections for the Reichstag, the Nazis win 107 seats. The party now drives ruthlessly for power, exploiting the fears of ordinary Germans that parliamentary government is not working and claiming that a strong line needs to be taken against communists.

**1932**
**April**       Hitler stands as a candidate in presidential election but is defeated by Hindenburg.
**July**        New elections. The Nazis win 230 seats and become the largest party in the Reichstag.
**November**    The Nazis lose ground in fresh elections, but remain the largest political party.

**1933**

**January**    Following unsuccessful manoeuvrings to find a new government, Hitler is appointed chancellor by President Hindenburg, in the hope that he can be controlled by other non-Nazi politicians.

**February**    Hitler announces new elections. The Nazis tighten their grip on government. When the Reichstag is burned down, a communist is blamed and the Communist Party is banned.

**March**    Elections confirm the Nazis as the largest party (288 seats), but they have to rely on the National People's Party to have a majority in the Reichstag. The Reichstag is opened (21 March) and almost immediately Hitler pushes through the Enabling Law, which gives the Nazi Party supreme power in Germany.

**April**    The first boycott of Jewish businesses takes place.

**July**    Germany is declared a one-party state.

**1934**

**30 June**    The 'Night of the Long Knives'. The SA leaders are eliminated, leaving Hitler free to build up links with the German army.

**2 August**    President Hindenburg dies. Hitler takes over the president's duties and declares himself 'Führer' (leader of the nation) and commander-in-chief of the German armed forces. The Nazis are now firmly in control of Germany.

# RESOURCES

**RECOMMENDED FURTHER READING**

**On the twentieth century:**

Tony Howarth, *Twentieth Century History: the world since 1900*, 2nd edition, Longman, 1987

J.A.S. Grenville, *The Collins History of the World in the Twentieth Century*, Harper-Collins, 1994

**On Hitler and other Nazi leaders:**

Klaus Fischer, *Nazi Germany: A New History*, Constable, 1995 (contains a useful reference section on the main Nazi leaders)

Norman Stone, *Hitler*, Coronet Books, 1989 (a short and well-written biography)

Joachim Fest, *Hitler*, Weidenfeld and Nicolson, 1974 (a longer biography)

Joachim Fest, *The Face of the Third Reich*, Penguin, 1979 (excellent insights into the background and personalities of the Nazi leaders

**On Weimar Germany and Hitler's rise:**

E. Feuchtwanger, *From Weimar to Hitler, Germany, 1918-1933*, Macmillan, 1995

C. Fischer, *The Rise of Hitler*, Manchester University Press, 1995 (a variety of documents are included at the end)

A. Nicholls, *Weimar and the Rise of Hitler*, 2nd edition, Macmillan, 1991

**FILMS**

There are many documentary accounts in film of the rise of Hitler and Nazi Germany. But, in particular, try to see Leni Riefenstahl's *The Triumph of the Will*, a propaganda film made of the 1934 Nuremberg rally.

# GLOSSARY

**anti-Semitism**    hatred of Jews. Anti-Semitism was a major force in the Nazi movement and eventually led to the Holocaust, the attempted extermination of European Jews.

**Aryan race**    Hitler claimed that the Germans were members of a superior race, the Aryans, who had been responsible for much of human progress and who thus deserved to dominate other peoples.

**chancellor**    the senior minister under the Weimar Constitution, appointed by the president.

**coalition government**    a government in which power is shared between a number of parties, usually because no one party has a majority.

**communism**    political belief that all goods in society should be shared equally. Communism was strong among German workers in 1929-32.

**coup**    a takeover of government, often through an armed uprising.

**fascism**    a political movement which grew up in Italy in the 1920s under the leadership of Benito Mussolini. The Fascists believed in strong government, the glorification of the nation, and an aggressive foreign policy.

**Freikorps**    groups of armed men established by the Weimar government to help keep order in the streets.

**Führer**    a leader (German). The term was used of Hitler, especially after he took the combined powers of chancellor and president in 1934.

**Gestapo**    the Nazi police force, first established in Prussia. Its job was to eliminate enemies of the state.

**great depression (economic)**    term used of the collapse in world trade and industry in 1929-32, which led to massive unemployment and unrest in many industrialized nations.

**inflation**    rising prices. If prices rise too fast, as in Germany in 1923, money becomes worthless.

**Mein Kampf ('My Struggle')**    book written by Hitler in 1924, in which he set out his ideas.

**Nazi**    shortened version of National Socialist German Workers' Party (Nationalsozialistische Deutsche Arbeiterpartei), Hitler's political party. The term 'Nazis' was used of Hitler's followers.

**president**    the most senior political figure, the figurehead of the nation. In the Weimar Republic the president was elected for seven years, and had wide political powers.

**proportional representation**    election system in which parties are awarded seats according to the number of votes they receive.

**Reichstag**    the German parliament.

**SA Sturmabteilung Stormtroopers**    Hitler's private army who kept order at meetings, beat up opponents and provided the massed ranks of Nazis at parades.

**SS Schutzstaffel**    originally Hitler's personal bodyguard, the SS became an instrument of terror responsible for many of the worst Nazi atrocities.

**swastika**    ancient symbol of good luck adopted by the Nazis as their emblem.

**Weimar Republic**    Germany's system of government, 1919-33. It was a democratic system centred on the Reichstag.

# INDEX

# SOURCES

The quotations in this book were taken from:

Alan Bullock, *Hitler: a Study in Tyranny*, Hamlyn, 1952

William Carr, *Hitler, a Study in Personality and Politics*, St Martin's, New York, 1979

Gordon Craig, *Germany, 1866-1945*, Oxford University Press, 1978

Joachim Fest, *Hitler*, Weidenfeld and Nicolson, 1974

Joachim Fest, *The Face of the Third Reich*, Penguin, 1979

E. Feuchtwanger, *From Weimar to Hitler, Germany, 1918-1933*, Macmillan, 1995

Klaus Fischer, *Nazi Germany: A New History*, Constable, 1995

*The Goebbels Diaries*, New York, 1948

F. Jetzinger, translated by Lawrence Wilson, *Hitler's Youth*, Hutchinson, 1958

P. Johnson, *A History of the Modern World*,

Weidenfeld and Nicolson, 1983

J. M. Keynes, *The Economic Consequences of the Peace*, 1921

Arthur Koestler, *The God that Failed*, Hamish Hamilton, 1949

Robert Lansing, *The Peace Negotiations*, 1921

K. Luedecke, *I Knew Hitler*, Jarrolds, 1938

Werner Maser, *Hitler*, Allen Lane, 1973

Milton Mayer, *They Thought They Were Free*, University of Chicago Press, 1955

P. Merkl, *Political Violence under the Swastika*, Princeton University Press, 1975

Gitta Sereny, *Albert Speer: His Battle with Truth*, Alfred Knopfler/Macmillan, 1995

William Shirer, *The Rise and Fall of the Third Reich*, Secker and Warburg, 1960

John Toland, *Hitler*, Doubleday, New York, 1976

Anthony Wood, *Europe 1815-1960*, Longman, 1986